Secrets of Efficient Game Development

By Marc Voxerton

Table of Contents

Author Introduction 4
Who this Book is for 5
General Concepts 6
    Introduction 7
    Why this is Important 8
    Cutting Corners vs Efficiency 9
    Hubris, the Enemy of Game Development 11
Art and 3D Modeling 12
    Introduction 13
    Art Options 14
    Base Mesh 16
    Retopology 19
    UV Unwrapping 24
    Workflow... 26
Coding 29
    Introduction 30
    Over Engineering 31
    Robust Systems 33
    Avoiding Similarities 34
Peer Pressure and Overthinking 35
    Managing External Pressure 36
    Overthinking too far into the Future 37
    Your reputation 38
General Tips 39
Contact the Author: 47

Author Introduction

My name is Marc (also known as SuperVoximus), and I've been making games for 17 years.

I have developed and published many games, ranging from small flash games in my youth, to casual mobile games, to large, multi-year ambitious games.

The very first tip I'll give you is to find creative ways to market your game, as I'm about to do.
My current main project is an Action Adventure game called Blade Of Ten, which at the time of writing this, has a free demo on steam! (See what I did there?)

I've worked alone for a lot of these projects, but I've also had quite a bit of experience with teams, both small and large. In fact, at the time of writing, I'm currently working with three different teams.

During this time, I've learned so many things about game development, particularly regarding where some of its greatest challenges lie. A part of me wishes I could go back in time to guide myself through this journey, which is why I'm writing this, in hopes to help fellow game developers navigate their path.

I will share with you all the things I consider valuable and important that I've learned regarding game development, with a focus on Indie/Solo game development. The main topic will be Efficiency, where we will learn to do things quickly, while retaining a maximum amount of quality and consistency.

Who this Book is for

The things I will share with you are meant to be most useful in solo projects or small indie teams, not AAA environments.

In most cases, AAA studios or large teams will prefer specialists who excel at a specific area of game development and adhere to certain standards and work pipelines. This means using industry standard programs and remaining within the well-structured confines of the work you were hired to do.

As an Indie Game Developer, or even more so, as a Solo Game Developer, a variety of skills can be more desirable. With limited resources and limited developers, efficiency and variety become a huge advantage.

AAA studios can afford to prioritize quality over efficiency, as they often employ hundreds of developers. As an Indie developer, doing that will cause one of two issues. Either you will have to scope down and change your vision, or your game will be tremendously delayed (or possibly never finished).

General Concepts

Table of Contents:

-Introduction
-Why this is Important
-Cutting Corners vs Efficiency
-Hubris, the Enemy of Game Development

Introduction

It's important to understand that Game Development Efficiency is not simply about speed, but about maximizing the investment that you make by giving you the best bang for your buck in terms of time and effort.

As an indie or solo game developer, your resources are limited, so they must be used in the most efficient manner possible to maximize the investment put into the project.
This will require you to sacrifice a certain amount of quality and precision, as it becomes increasingly difficult to improve your work after you've reached a certain point.
The problem with mastery of a skill is diminishing returns. This doesn't matter if your goal is to achieve mastery, as you would follow a straight path until you've accomplished this goal.
However, if your goal is to make (and finish) a game, especially with limited resources, time becomes a scant resource of incredible value.
Quality is still an important component of efficiency, it's about allocating resources in an advantageous manner. This is even more important when you are a generalist or a solo developer attempting to juggle all aspects of game development.
Being a generalist is no easy task, it's essentially doing many jobs at once, but being efficient can help you balance all of it out to accomplish your goals.

Why this is Important

Games take a really long time to make. Sometimes, they take a really, really, really long time to make.
 In many cases, you must make thousands of assets, write hundreds of scripts, animate countless walk cycles, compose music, make effects, balance your game and write an entire story by yourself or with a small team.
The popular solution to this has historically been to lower your scope and make a game that is smaller than you would like, which isn't always a bad thing. But what if you wanted to make the game you envision in all of its glory? Without cutting any content, without changing the core essence of what makes it special?
This only becomes possible by giving something up in return. Even if you possessed the most incredible mind in history, and the world's most impressive work ethic, mastering and applying all the skills needed to make a game to their fullest extent would still not be feasible due to time constraints.
A question to ask yourself would be "how important is X to my game?"
Give elements that you want to incorporate into your game a value of importance before tackling them.
For example, it's very important for me to have nice looking armor in my game, but it's not really necessary for the armor to have advanced physics.
I can then invest the time to design nice looking armor, and instead of spending time on adding advanced armor physics, I can spend it on something else and make more progress.

Cutting Corners vs Efficiency

There's a big difference between being efficient and selective about your time, and cutting corners. Cutting corners aims to reduce your investment, while being efficient does so under the condition that you are still maintaining a certain standard of quality.

A general rule of thumb is that the more time you put into something, it will take more and more time to improve it throughout that process.

For example, a product that is 2/10 on the quality scale can be improved to a 7/10 with minimal effort, but a product that is an 8/10 would take a huge amount of effort to reach a 9/10.

It's much more efficient to put in 2 hours to get to a 7/10 in quality, than putting in 20 hours to reach a 9/10. Most people will barely notice the difference unless they have a trained eye.

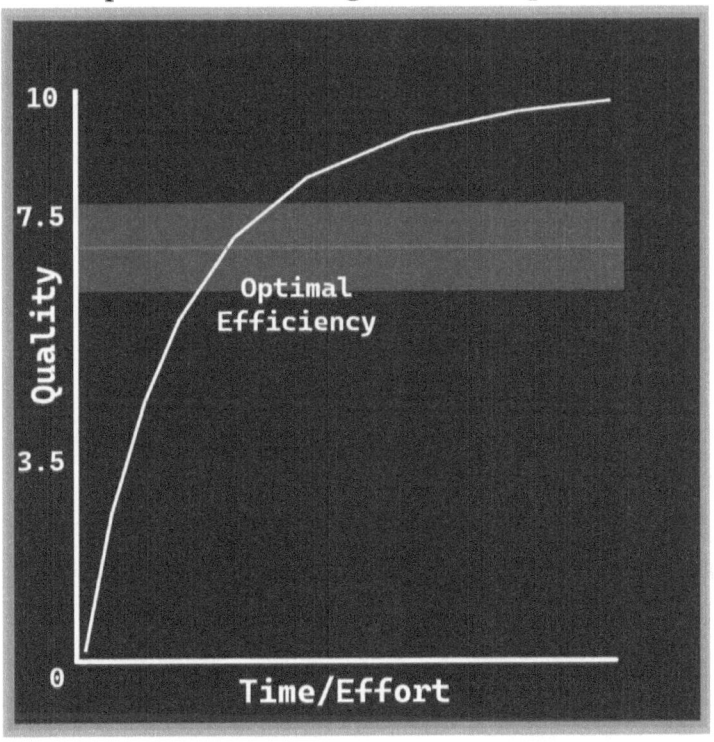
Graph demonstrating diminishing returns

Hubris, the Enemy of Game Development

Striving for excellence is a great thing, and having pride in our work and accomplishments is understandable, but we must be careful not to lose sight of the main goal we are after, which is usually making a great game.
In this industry, many people will judge you for not doing things the "right way", which may make sense in a AAA environment or in some sort of large, structured, compartmentalized team.
But at the end of the day, if you're making your own game, there is no need to adhere to strict guidelines unless it benefits you.
We're not doctors, or architects, or rocket scientists, we're game developers.
Laser precision in your work is not needed to make a good game. While game development is a highly technical field, it's also primarily a form of art, capable of nuance in both its expression and its inner workings.
As long as your game works the way you want it to work, and it runs smoothly, then that's all that really matters (if you're working with a team, it's also important to make sure others can work with your code and assets in a streamlined way).
If your goal is to make a good game, then don't get caught up in an elitist mentality, as it will hold you back by enticing you to focus your energy where it is not directly needed to achieve your goals.

Next up, we'll take a look at some ways to achieve efficiency in game design using concrete and practical examples.

Art and 3D Modeling

Table of Contents:

- Introduction
- Art Options
- Base Mesh
- Retopology
- UV Unwrapping
- Workflow

Introduction

Art is an important part of a video game. I have great respect for all artists and the techniques they use to achieve great results. There are many amazing things that artists do to make things look good, but I'm going to make a case against using some of them.
This may be controversial, but once again, the aim here is efficiency, not perfection. We want to maximize the amount of quality we get for the least amount of investment.

This section is in no way discrediting fundamental art techniques or suggesting substitutions for them, but rather offering different paths to take for the specific cases where developers need to be efficient with their work. (If your goal is to be a professional artist, this is not the approach for you!)

We will discuss ways you can speed up your workflow while minimizing quality loss. We will also quantify the potential importance of managing your workflow by comparing time to money and simulating a few different cases.

Art Options

When art is involved, there are a few different options that a developer can look at for efficiency. Usually your options consist of the following.

```
A: Make the art yourself
B: Hire someone to make art
C: Buy art assets (Use sparingly)
D: Use AI to generate art assets (Highly
Discouraged)
```

A is a great option in most cases, you can save money, and using some of the techniques described in this book, you can save time as well. Making your own assets gives you a clear conscience and pride in your hard work. That being said, this is by far the most time consuming option, as it is a huge part of making a game. This option is also by far the most receptive to the topics discussed in this book.

B can also be great if you can afford it. If you're a solo developer, or if you have a small studio, it may be difficult to secure the budget for an artist. Having a dedicated artist would save you time and can guarantee a standard of quality, however it's not always possible to work with an artist depending on your situation.

C is where things get a bit complicated. Some assets are great and can be a wonderful addition to your game. Art packs, for example, can be very useful, save you a bunch of time and fit right into your game. However, oftentimes, premade assets will stand out from the rest of the assets in your game, as they were not meant to fit the look and feel of your game specifically. Whether you're comparing these to assets you made yourself, or assets you've acquired from someone else, every artist has their own style, workflow, technique and vision in mind which plays a big role in how well the asset integrates.

Furthermore, it's important to use assets sparingly, to avoid a lack of cohesiveness and creativity (take asset flip games as an example on what not to do).

Finally, make sure the license for the asset allows you to use it in the context you want to use it in.

D should be avoided at all costs unless you are doing some sort of experimental personal project that won't be released.

AI generated assets are more than often heavily lacking in quality and come with an array of potential copyright/legal issues. AI models are often trained on public works done by other people, which can create issues, as well as being morally questionable in certain cases.

Base Mesh

Creating a base mesh is one of the most valuable things you can do, especially if your game contains a lot of similar characters (mostly humans, mostly wolves etc).

A base mesh can serve as a sort of template that you can use for multiple characters. For example, I start with a generic humanoid base mesh for my human characters. This works because the base mesh has elements that many of my characters share. Why would you model a hand three hundred times when you can do it once, then tweak it to fit your character?

This may give the impression that all characters would look the same, but this is not true. Using a generic looking humanoid base mesh, I'm able to make characters such as aliens, demons, elves, monsters, weird insect-people with blades for arms and more. The base mesh covers repetitive and non creative tasks that you would have to do over and over again for no good reason, it should not restrict your creativity, but support it.

In most cases, it would be a good idea to attempt to remain within the loose confines of the base mesh, as it will yield better results. For example, you should try to only use humanoid base meshes for humanoid adjacent characters. You can break this rule, but it defeats the purpose of having a base mesh, as you will have to remodel large portions of it anyways.

Base Mesh and some examples of characters that derived from it

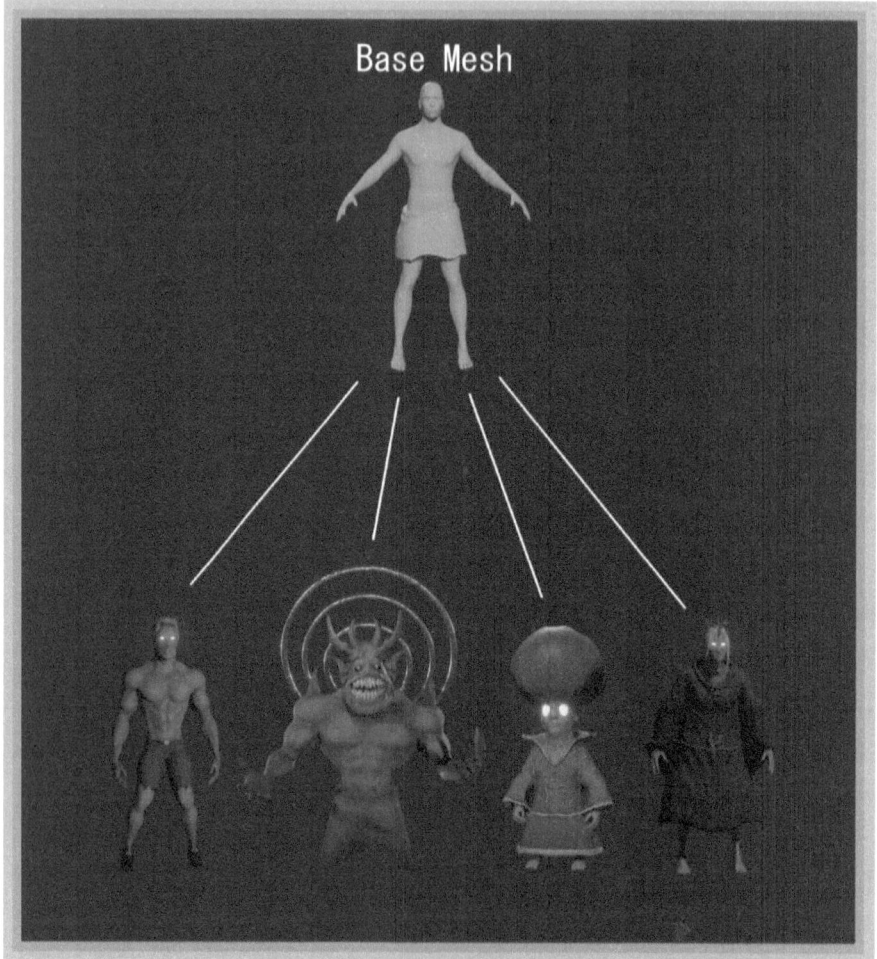

We can see the amount of variety one can derive from a single, generic, humanoid base mesh. This particular one was made using MakeHuman. The conclusion is that the base mesh does not really limit the amount of variation and creativity that can be expressed.

Let's do some math to demonstrate how much time you can save by using a base mesh. In my game, Blade Of Ten, I probably have around one hundred characters that have been made from a humanoid base mesh.

```
Assuming:
-100 3D models
-5 hours per base mesh
-5*100 = 500 hours
(20$/h wage: 10,000$)
```

That's five hundred hours saved. If you were getting paid twenty dollars an hour for this time, it would be worth ten thousand dollars!

Saving time isn't the only thing a base mesh is good for, it also helps ensure cohesiveness and consistency with your art. Draw or model a basketball on ten different occasions and you will find that it will be slightly different every time. The position or curvature of the lines may differ, the size or proportions may differ, it will never be the same.
Similarly, making many characters from scratch may give you a discrepancy in proportion or style, while using a base mesh guides you towards more controlled and desirable deviations. You could even set up rigs for the base mesh, some UVs or anything you feel like you will reuse to an extent.
The goal is to eliminate non-creative and repetitive elements from your workflow in order to make more space for creative elements.
Think of it this way, imagine if you had to code a 3D modeling program every single time you wanted to create a new character, you would never get anything done. Obviously this is an extreme example, however it demonstrates the idea under a different perspective.

Retopology

Another art technique that can be quite time consuming is retopology.
Retopology is a technique where you essentially refactor your mesh in a more optimized fashion. This is useful for a number of things.

```
-Performance: By lowering the polygon
count.

-Mesh manipulation: Working with your mesh
becomes easier when the topology is clean
and uniform.

-Better rigging: Rigging will be easier and
more effective with good topology.

-Better UV mapping: UV mapping will be
quicker and more straightforward when your
topology allows easy access to seams.
```

Retopology takes time, but can often be worth it. I'm going to make a case against it, however this should be taken with a grain of salt as depending on your situation and your workflow, you may benefit from manual retopology. This section is mostly going to be pertaining to the performance aspects of retopology, rather than functionality.

In my case, I generally get certain things like UV mapping and rigging done on my base mesh or early on in the process, before I subdivide my mesh or add details. When I am using this process, retopology mostly gives me performance incentives. I can spend hours retopologizing a model and get the best quality, or I can use Blender's decimate modifier and cut my polycount down in mere seconds (and expect lower quality).

The question here is whether the increased quality of manual retopology is worth the 12 hours spent doing it or not. The answer depends on a few factors such as how big your team is, how many models you need for your game, what your workflow is like, how important visual fidelity is for your game, how close the camera in your game will be etc. In most cases as a solo developer, I wouldn't manually retopologize a model.

In my game Blade Of Ten, I have hundreds of characters and thousands of 3D models. Let's do some math.

```
Assuming:
-300 3D models to retopologize
-Average of 5 hours of retopology per model
-300 x 5 = 1,500 hours
(20$/h wage: 30,000$)
```

That's one thousand five hundred hours saved and that have been spent on other things in the game. This time would technically be worth thirty thousand dollars assuming you are earning twenty dollars an hour.

The drawback? Some inconvenience and slightly lower quality meshes that are basically indiscernible from what they would have looked like if they had been retopologized manually. If I had used those ten thousand hours just on retopology, the game would not even be remotely close to release, and the investment would not be worth it.

Let's take a look at what kind of quality differences we can notice with retopology vs decimation (or similar tools).

Subdivided mesh vs Retopology vs Decimation

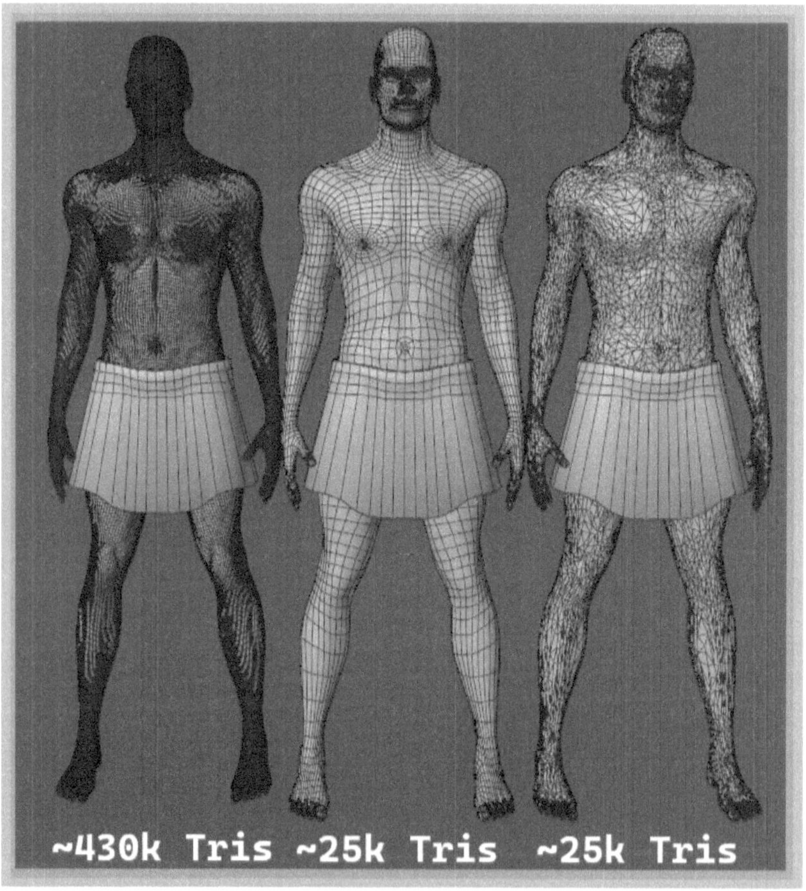

To be fully clear and transparent, retopology absolutely yields better results than decimation. We can see that decimation gives us an absolute mess of a topology, which comes with an array of issues and obstacles.

However, let's look at these meshes side by side, without the wireframe.

Subdivided mesh vs Retopology vs Decimation (No wireframe)

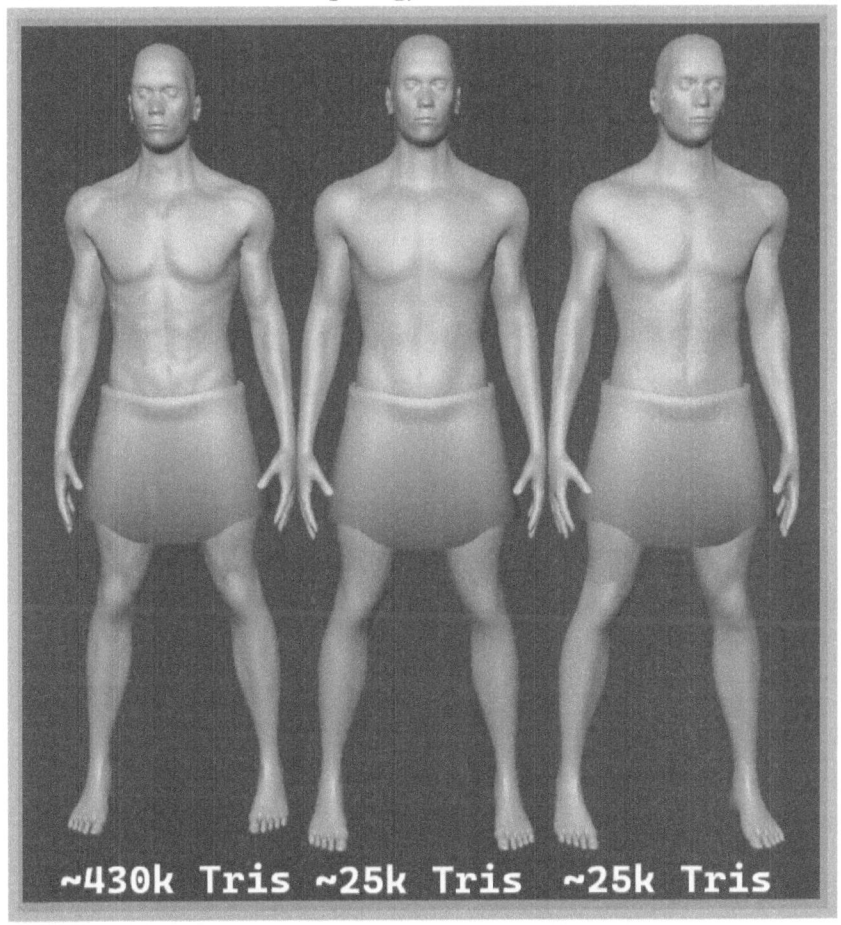

While we notice a considerable difference in detail between the subdivided mesh and the other two, there is virtually no visual difference between retopology and decimation in this case.

Bad topology should not be encouraged, but if your workflow allows for it with limited drawbacks (for example by UV unwrapping and rigging was done prior to decimation to limit the damage), then it can be a viable option to make best use of your time.

Auto retopology, decimation or similar tools are indeed a form of automation, however they are non-creative in nature.

They only affect the presentation of your mesh (often not significant enough to warrant discarding) and do not affect the actual design of your mesh.

It can be easy to get caught up in the technicalities and the idea of doing things the standard way, however I find that breaking things down into simple terms can help guide me to deciding my approach.

In this particular case, using automated tools to cut down polygons gives me very similar results, and not enough inconvenience to bother me, therefore I opt for this option to save time and effort for other things.

UV Unwrapping

UV unwrapping allows us to map faces from our mesh to a texture. Depending on how the mesh is unwrapped, the quality of your texture can vary immensely. Good UVs may, for example, allocate more pixels for important or large parts of the mesh. This allows us to represent more detail in important parts of the mesh.

I cannot stress this enough, avoid unwrapping after decimating (if you choose to decimate). Decimation, or similar modifiers will distort your topology immensely, making it much, much more difficult to unwrap effectively, whether you do it manually or automatically.

In order to efficiently unwrap a mesh, good topology would be ideal, but you can still achieve acceptable results as long as your topology isn't horrible.

Let's do a bit more math to support automatic UV Unwrapping using Blade of Ten as an example.

```
Assuming:
-300 3D models
-3 hours per UV map
-3*300 = 900 hours
(20$/h wage: 13,000$)
```

Another nine hundred hours saved, which would be worth thirteen thousand dollars. It's important to note that unwrapping time can vary greatly based on experience and the type of mesh you're working with.

In total, we would have saved:

```
-2900 hours
-5 hours per base mesh
-53,000$
```

That's a lot of hours and a lot of dollars to end up with comparable visual results. As a solo/indie game developer, this is incredibly valuable.
Now of course, the money is only a representation of the time spent, so while you are not earning fifty three thousand dollars, you are saving time and effort equivalent to that.

It's worth mentioning that automatic UVs aren't usually good enough right out of the box, but they can be edited. I often use automatic UVs and make a few changes, for example giving my character's most important parts more space on the texture for higher resolution, or adjusting spacing to avoid overlapping UVs.

We will now go over workflows and how the entire process could look while utilizing these techniques. I have personally had pretty good results using this workflow and I've found that, through time, you may be able to tweak it gradually to accommodate your own preferences.
Remember, these are just ideas, and not guidelines, the entire point is to do whatever works best for you and your work style.

Workflow

My usual workflow usually follows these steps.

```
Base mesh > Modify > Rig/Unwrap >
Subdivide/Sculpt > Decimate and Bake
normals
```

Base mesh: Start with a base mesh, ideally with a basic rig set up tailored to my goals, sometimes already UV mapped. You can make your own, or you can use a premade one as long as you have the correct rights for it.

I've made some from scratch and I've made some using external programs, my advice is to try and go for a very generic and bland design. Think of a blank canvas, the more devoid of direction it is, the more variety it will allow. Another consideration is the art direction you want to take (you may want specific, cartoonish proportions for example, it could be a good idea to have a base mesh for that specific purpose).

Modify: If I need to add elements such as extra arms, horns or anything that requires creation of geometry, I try to do all of it first, as it will affect rigging and UV mapping. This part is mostly related to polygonal modeling, adding or removing elements and mapping out the general design of the mesh.

Rig/Unwrap: If my base mesh doesn't have these, or if I modified the geometry, I rig and unwrap before the topology gets too complex.

Subdivide/Sculpt: I then subdivide to get a higher polygonal density to allow for better sculpting, this is where the details come in. Sculpting without enough polygon density will not be effective, so I try to aim for at least four hundred thousand polygons for a character (could be more or less for other types of meshes).

You can sculpt with a mouse, although I find a pen to be very effective and easier on the wrists. If you feel like you could benefit from a pen and tablet, consider getting an affordable one and giving it a try.

At this point I generally texture the model as well, using the details of my sculpt to guide my texturing.

Decimate and bake normals: This is where I duplicate my high resolution mesh, decimate the original, then I use the high resolution copy to bake normals onto the decimated mesh. This allows you to retain some of the details from your high resolution sculpt, while cutting down the polygon count.

Normal maps essentially save geometrical data onto a texture, which can then be plugged into your material. It gives the illusion of geometry, without actually creating geometry, which I find to be quite useful.

I then begin animating, which can be made to be more efficient by reusing animations and practicing to develop some muscle memory for similar animations (walk, run, hit etc are all animations that could follow similar steps that can be built using muscle memory, allowing you to make them faster with time).

By having an established workflow that I am used to, I can be more efficient, and muscle memory helps a lot with that. It's important to note that you should use a workflow that works for you, as some people may have different preferences. If something gives you good results and helps you be more efficient, I encourage you to do it, even if it doesn't align with the techniques described in this book.

Coding

Table of Contents:

-Introduction
-Over Engineering
-Robust Systems
-Avoiding Similarities

Introduction

When it comes to coding, efficiency will look different based on what kind of project you're working on and how complex it is.

In general, when you are working on a large project, it's important to invest in a robust and reliable way of coding. This allows you to do a lot of the work up front to avoid future hiccups.
When you are working on a relatively smaller project, you can afford to be a bit more lenient with yourself in certain ways if it helps speed up the process.
For example, it wouldn't make much sense to create a fully developed inventory system if your game only makes use of a singular item you collect, that would just be a waste of resources.

If your game uses hundreds of items however, it is paramount to have a robust inventory system to reduce the amount of hiccups you encounter each time you need to use this system.

Over Engineering

Over engineering is when a simple problem is handled in an unnecessarily complex manner. Sometimes this is due to worrying about features that we might need in the future, which is understandable. Other times it's because we've been conditioned to think that it's always the way to go, which shouldn't be the case.
I see this too often, over engineering and overcomplicating your code can hinder progress, especially if you are working with others. Simplicity is the sign of good code, as it allows you to get your game up and running without having to navigate through a complicated maze of algorithms when you want to make changes. This is even more true when you are working with others, even if your code is objectively more performant and provides better reliability, sometimes it is not worth it to spend hours and hours on a script that won't be very consequential.

Once again, it's important to remember that it is objectively better to write good and proper code in most cases, even more so in professional AAA environments, but the whole point of this book is to find ways to be efficient as a developer with limited resources.
I like to think of it as going to a fancy restaurant and ordering a burger. They might bring out this overly complicated burger with caviar, truffle shavings and other exotic ingredients as toppings, which is objectively more impressive than making a simple burger, but what about the taste? Sure, sometimes these burgers taste great, and there's certainly a time and place for them, but in

most cases, people will prefer a good quality, simple, classic burger.

Robust Systems

Time for some contradiction!
On the other hand, when dealing with systems that will be constantly reused throughout your game, such as an inventory system, or an NPC system, the opposite of what was mentioned in the previous section is usually true. It is paramount to have these fundamental systems set up in a way that will make your life easier down the line.
I use the inventory system in Blade of Ten constantly, through quests, combat, mining, fishing and more. It makes sense to "over engineer" such a system to avoid headaches in the future. Spending the extra fifty hours to make sure I can seamlessly manipulate items in the game will save me hundreds of hours as I go through the development process.
This is because of frequent use.

Comparing it to food again, it's like preparing a big batch of chopped garlic and freezing it for later use. Very laborious initially, but if you use chopped garlic in a lot of your dishes, you'll save lots of time in the future.

Another example, would you pay ten thousand dollars for a car only to use it once? It would be much more economically viable to just take a cab. But if you had to commute to work every day, buying a car would save you money down the line.

Avoiding Similarities

Sometimes we have mechanics in our games that act quite similar. For example, a door script that teleports you to a different area, and a door script that loads you into a whole different scene. Instead of having copious amounts of scripts that share much of the same logic (collision, conditions for entering the door etc), these can be merged into a single door script, with parameters that you can define later on to let the game know what kind of door it is.

Peer Pressure and Overthinking

Table of Contents:

-Introduction
-Managing External Pressure
-Overthinking too Far into the Future
-Your Reputation

Managing External Pressure

You will most likely be bombarded with information, advice and criticism. People will expect you to do things the way they were taught to do things or to adhere to certain practices.
It's up to you to parse this information in a way that suits your needs, so my advice is to trust your judgement, but be open to input.
When it comes to choosing the right information, it's always a good idea to break it down into fundamental ideas and remind yourself of a clear goal that you set for yourself.

For example: "I want to work at a AAA game studio" would imply that you should learn the practices and workflows that are favored by these studios to increase your chances of getting hired.
On the other hand: "I want to make a great game" would imply that your efforts should be geared towards making a great game no matter if people disagree with how you do it.

At the end of the day, it's all about your personal goals and what you want to achieve. Having these conversations in your mind can help you make important decisions that will shape your workflow significantly.

Overthinking too far into the Future

I've seen this particularly in game developers who are just starting out, although it exists with more experienced developers as well.

When making a game, it's natural to want to figure out how you're going to approach the entire process carefully before you invest too much of your time and effort.

Imagine putting in hundreds of hours only to be met with some insurmountable obstacle... I'd be lying if I said I never suffered from such anxious thoughts myself, but overly worrying about this paralyzes us and halts progress.

A good way to get around this type of anxiety, at least for me, was to make small games that I actually finished and published. We've all been there, having a huge amount of unfinished projects sitting on some old HDD is quite common amongst game developers. The problem with this is that it prevents developers from acquiring key experiences from late stage game development.

Preparing a game for release, dealing with paperwork, marketing and post launch bug fixes are examples of things developers may worry about at the beginning of the development cycle.

My advice is to get that experience from small projects and not to dwell on it much. Game development is an arduous journey filled with obstacles and challenges, it is paramount to get comfortable with facing challenges.

A certain amount of confidence and self belief is required for success, which can be practiced and built no matter how little of it you feel like you have.

Your reputation

Let's be real, following some of the ideas outlined in this book could make quite a bit of people judge and question your reputation as a professional developer. I don't always blame people who do this, because I can see where they're coming from. But my goal is to make the games that I envision, which are often large in scale. When I describe my game to developers, I'm often met with reactions such as "you're overscoping, you need to control how big your game is so you actually finish it", which is generally pretty good advice in most cases. In fact, I give this same advice quite often, however, by prioritizing efficiency, I'm able to produce content at a much, much faster rate than expected, and because of that, my game is nearing completion regardless of its scale.

Since I know that this is working for me personally, then I'm okay with people disagreeing with how I do things. Those kinds of decisions will boil down to your priorities and goals, just be sure not to let others dictate your path for you.

Thank you for reading! In the next section, you'll find a variety of random tips, tricks and some trivia on game development.

General Tips

1:

Blender is a free 3D modeling software, capable of modeling, sculpting, animating, texturing and more!

2:

Some popular game engines include Unity, Unreal Engine and Godot.

3:

To visualize UV unwrapping, imagine cutting the edges of a cardboard box without (without separating the cardboard) and laying it down flat.

4:

Sculpting is significantly easier and more effective if you have a high polygon count.

5:

Polygon counts can be lowered, using retopology, decimation or similar tools/techniques.

6:
The reason polygon counts need to be lowered is to improve performance.

7:
Detail can be preserved even in meshes with a lowered polycount by using a normal map.

8:
A huge part of optimizing your code is recognizing operations and calculations that are computationally heavy.

9:
Avoid putting computationally heavy code in Update functions (functions that run very often or every frame).

10:
Normal maps react to light in your scene, so the detail may not look like what you expect in the shade.

11:
Want to make things glow? Try adding an emission map!

12:
Emission maps don't look flat? Try adding some bloom!

13:
LODs (Level Of Detail) allow you to switch between different versions of a mesh based on its distance from the camera.

14:
LODs lower the quality of your mesh the farther it is from the camera because the loss of detail is harder to notice from a distance.

15:
Audacity is a free audio editing and recording program that lets you record and edit sound effects, voice lines and more.

16:
There are many good DAWs (digital audio workstation), LMMS is a free one.

17:
If automatic UV unwrapping is giving you overlapping seams, try increasing the island margin a bit.

18:
Modeling hair can be challenging, but there are many effective ways to do it, such as using hair cards, polygonal modeling or curves.

19:
Cutout materials let you make parts of a texture invisible.

20:
You can use cutout materials to simulate very dense meshes, for example, bits of fur on a jacket.

21:
If you're just starting out, try making some very small games at first, before tackling a larger project.

22:
If you're working with a team, it's important to make sure your code is easy to read and understand.

23:
An easy base for modeling clothes could be duplicating parts of the body (torso, legs etc), making them larger and editing them.

24:
Post processing can really help your scene pop and look better.

25:
Backface culling disables rendering of the back side of a face, this is to save performance, as in most cases.

26:
When assembling a team, take into consideration people's personalities instead focusing solely on their skills.

27:
Don't burn yourself out, your health is more important than making progress on your game, and you'll make better progress if you are well rested anyways.

28:
Do your best to meet your needs outside of game development, as they will affect your wellbeing and performance.

29:
Finishing a game is an achievement in and of itself, don't be hard on yourself if your game isn't as well received as you had hoped.

30:
Play games for inspiration when you aren't feeling as motivated as you usually do.

31:
Always believe in yourself! It makes a world of a difference.

32:
Watching your favorite developers work (if they stream or make videos) can help you learn new techniques.

33:
Use profiling tools to determine what's causing bottlenecks if you're having performance issues.

34:
Join game development discords to make like-minded friends, learn new things and network.

35:
Pay attention to the scope of your game to make sure you're in control of what you want to create.

36:
Games don't need to be a certain way, some games focus on gameplay, others focus on cinematics, or storytelling, or visuals. They all have their own value.

37:
Billboarding involves having a texture on a flat surface that always faces the camera. This is useful for performance when making far away objects or things like vegetation.

38:
Frustum culling disables rendering for objects that are outside of a camera's field of a vision,

39:
Distance culling disables rendering for objects that are far away.

40:
To mask the jarring nature of distance culling, you can add fog as a sort of buffer zone.

Contact the Author:
Marc Voxerton

Email: Supergamedeveloper96@gmail.com
Discord: SuperVoximus
Instagram: SuperVoximus
X: SuperVoximus
Bluesky: SuperVoximus
Youtube: SuperVoximus
Twitch: SuperVoximus

www.ingramcontent.com/pod-product-compliance
Lightning Source LLC
Chambersburg PA
CBHW030516220526
45464CB00006B/2822